This was the king's semi-barbaric method of administering justice.

Its perfect fairness is obvious.

CREATIVE SHORT STORIES

THE LADY, OR THE TIGER?

FRANK STOCKTON

CREATIVE EDUCATION

THE LADY, OR THE TIGER?

I n the very olden time there lived a semi-barbaric king, whose ideas, though somewhat polished and sharpened by the progressiveness of distant Latin neighbors, were still large, florid, and untrammelled, as became the half of him which was barbaric. He was a man of exuberant fancy, and, withal, of an authority so irresistible that, at his will, he turned his varied fancies into facts. He was greatly given to self-communing; and when he and himself agreed upon anything, the thing was done. When every member of his domestic and political systems moved smoothly in its appointed course, his nature was bland and genial; but whenever there was a little hitch, and some of his orbs got out of their orbits, he was blander and more genial still, for nothing pleased him so much as to make the crooked straight, and crush down uneven places.

Among the borrowed notions by which his barbarism had become semified was that of the public arena, in which, by exhibitions of manly and beastly valor, the minds of his subjects were refined and cultured.

But even here the exuberant and barbaric fancy asserted itself. The arena of the king was built, not to give the people an opportunity of hearing the rhapsodies of dying gladiators, nor to enable them to view the inevitable conclusion of a conflict between religious opinions and hungry jaws, but for purposes far better adapted to widen and develop the mental energies of the people. This vast amphitheater, with its encircling galleries, its mysterious vaults, and its unseen passages, was an agent of poetic justice, in which crime was punished, or virtue rewarded, by the decrees of an impartial and incorruptible chance.

When a subject was accused of a crime of sufficient importance to interest the king, public notice was given that on an appointed day the fate of the accused person would be decided in the king's arena—a structure which well deserved its name; for, although its form and plan were borrowed from afar, its purpose emanated solely from the brain of this man, who, every barleycorn a king, knew no tradition to which he owed more allegiance than pleased his fancy, and who ingrafted on every adopted form of human thought and action the rich growth of his barbaric idealism.

When all the people had assembled in the galleries, and the king, surrounded by his court, sat high up on his throne of royal state on one side of the arena, he gave a signal, a door beneath him opened, and the accused subject stepped out into the amphitheater. Directly opposite him, on the other side of the enclosed space, were two doors, exactly alike and side by side. It was the duty and the privilege of the person on trial to walk directly to these doors and open one of them. He could open either door he pleased: he was subject to no guidance or influence but that of the aforementioned impartial and incorruptible chance. If he opened the one, there came out of it a hungry tiger, the fiercest and most cruel that could be procured, which immediately sprang upon him and tore him to pieces, as a punishment for his guilt. The moment that the case of the criminal was thus decided, doleful iron bells were clanged, great wails went up from the hired mourners posted on the outer rim of the arena, and the vast audience, with bowed heads and downcast hearts, wended slowly their homeward way, mourning greatly that one so young and fair, or so old and respected, should have merited so dire a fate.

But if the accused person opened the other door, there came forth from it a lady, the most suitable to his years and station that his Majesty could select among his fair subjects; and to this lady he was immediately married, as a reward of his innocence. It mattered not that he might already possess a wife and family, or that his affections might be engaged upon an object of his own selection: the king allowed no such subordinate arrangements to interfere with his great scheme of retribution and reward. The exercises, as in the other instance, took place immediately, and in the arena. Another door opened beneath the king, and a priest, followed by a band of choristers, and dancing maidens blowing joyous airs on golden horns and treading an epithalamic measure, advanced to where the pair stood side by side; and the wedding was promptly and cheerily solemnized. Then the gay brass bells rang forth their merry peals, the people shouted glad hurrahs, and the innocent man, preceded by children strewing flowers on his path, led his bride to his home.

This was the king's semi-barbaric method of administering justice. Its perfect fairness is obvious. The criminal could not know out of which door would come the lady: he opened either he pleased, without having the slightest idea whether, in the next instant, he was to be devoured or married. On some occasions the tiger came out of one door, and on some out of the other. The decisions of this tribunal were not only fair, they were positively determinate: the accused person was instantly punished if he found himself guilty; and if innocent, he was rewarded on the spot, whether he liked it or not. There was no escape from the judgments of the king's arena.

The institution was a very popular one. When the people gathered together on one of the great trial-days, they never knew whether they were to witness a bloody slaughter or a hilarious wedding. This element of uncertainty lent an interest to the occasion which it could not otherwise have attained. Thus the masses were entertained and pleased, and the thinking part of the community could bring no charge of unfairness against this plan; for did not the accused person have the whole matter in his own hands?

This semi-barbaric king had a daughter as blooming as his most florid fancies, and with a soul as fervent and imperious as his own. As is usual in such cases, she was the apple of his eye, and was loved by him above all humanity. Among his courtiers was a young man of that fineness of blood and lowness of station common to the conventional heroes of romance who love royal maidens. This royal maiden was well satisfied with her lover, for he was handsome and brave to a degree unsurpassed in all this kingdom; and she loved him with an ardor that had enough of barbarism in it to make it exceedingly warm and strong. This love affair moved on happily for many months, until one day the king happened to discover its existence. He did not hesitate nor waver in regard to his duty in the premises. The youth was immediately cast into prison, and a day was appointed for his trial in the king's arena. This, of course, was an especially important occasion; and his Majesty, as well as all the people, was greatly interested in the workings and development of this trial. Never before had such a case occurred; never before had a subject dared to love the daughter of a king. In after years such things became common-place enough; but then they were, in no slight degree, novel and startling.

The tiger-cages of the kingdom were searched for the most savage and relentless beasts, from which the fiercest monster might be selected for the arena; and the ranks of maiden youth and beauty throughout the land were carefully surveyed by competent judges, in order that the young man might have a fitting bride in case fate did not determine for him a different destiny. Of course, everybody knew that the deed with which the accused was charged had been done. He had loved the princess, and neither he, she, nor any one else thought of denying the fact; but the king would not think of allowing any fact of this kind to interfere with the workings of the tribunal, in which he took such great delight and satisfaction. No matter how the affair turned out, the youth would be disposed of; and the king would take an aesthetic pleasure in watching the course of events, which would determine whether or not the young man had done wrong in allowing himself to love the princess.

The appointed day arrived. From far and near the people gathered, and thronged the great galleries of the arena; and crowds, unable to gain admittance, massed themselves against its outside walls. The king and his court were in their places, opposite the twin doors—those fateful portals, so terrible in their similarity.

All was ready. The signal was given. A door beneath the royal party opened, and the lover of the princess walked into the arena. Tall, beautiful, fair, his appearance was greeted with a low hum of admiration and anxiety. Half the audience had not known so grand a youth had lived among them. No wonder the princess loved him! What a terrible thing for him to be there!

As the youth advanced into the arena, he turned, as the custom was, to bow to the king: but he did not think at all of that royal personage; his eyes were fixed upon the princess, who sat to the right of her father. Had it not been for the moiety of barbarism in her nature, it is probable that lady would not have been there; but her intense and fervid soul would not allow her to be absent on an occasion in which she was so terribly interested. From the moment that the decree had gone forth, that her lover should decide his fate in the king's arena, she had thought of nothing, night or day, but this great event and the various subjects connected with it. Possessed of more power, influence, and force of character than anyone who had ever before been interested in such a case, she had done what no other person had done—she had possessed herself of the secret of the doors. She knew in which of the two rooms that lay behind those doors stood the cage of the tiger, with its open front, and in which waited the lady. Through these thick doors, heavily curtained with skins on the inside, it was impossible that any noise or suggestion should come from within to the person who should approach to raise the latch of one of them; but gold, and the power of a woman's will, had brought the secret to the princess.

And not only did she know in which room stood the lady ready to emerge, all blushing and radiant, should her door be opened, but she knew who the lady was. It was one of the fairest and loveliest of the damsels of the court who had been selected as the reward of the accused youth, should he be proved innocent of the crime of aspiring to one so far above him; and the princess hated her. Often had she seen, or imagined that she had seen, this fair creature throwing glances of admiration upon the person of her lover, and sometimes she thought these glances were perceived and even returned. Now and then she had seen them talking together; it was but for a moment or two, but much can be said in a brief space; it may have been on most unimportant topics, but how could she know that? The girl was lovely, but she had dared to raise her eyes to the loved one of the princess; and, with all the intensity of the savage blood transmitted to her through long lines of wholly barbaric ancestors, she hated the woman who blushed and trembled behind that silent door.

When her lover turned and looked at her, and his eye met hers as she sat there paler and whiter than anyone in the vast ocean of anxious faces about her, he saw, by that power of quick perception which is given to those whose souls are one, that she knew behind which door crouched the tiger, and behind which stood the lady. He had expected her to know it. He understood her nature, and his soul was assured that she would never rest until she had made plain to herself this thing, hidden to all other lookers-on, even to the king. The only hope for the youth in which there was any element of certainty was based upon the success of the princess in discovering this mystery; and the moment he looked upon her, he saw she had succeeded, as in his soul he knew she would succeed.

Then it was that his quick and anxious glance asked the question, "Which?" It was as plain to her as if he shouted it from where he stood. There was not an instant to be lost. The question was asked in a flash; it must be answered in another.

Her right arm lay on the cushioned parapet before her. She raised her hand, and made a slight, quick movement toward the right. No one but her lover saw her. Every eye but his was fixed on the man in the arena.

He turned, and with a firm and rapid step he walked across the empty space. Every heart stopped beating, every breath was held, every eye was fixed immovably upon that man. Without the slightest hesitation, he went to the door on the right, and opened it.

Now, the point of the story is this: Did the tiger come out of that door, or did the lady?

The more we reflect upon this question, the harder it is to answer. It involves a study of the human heart which leads us through devious mazes of passion, out of which it is difficult to find our way. Think of it,

fair reader, not as if the decision of the question depended upon yourself,

but upon that hot-blooded, semi-barbaric princess, her soul at a white heat

beneath the combined fires of despair and jealousy. She had lost him, but

who should have him?

How often, in her waking hours and in her dreams, had she start-

ed in wild horror, and covered her face with her hands as she thought of

her lover opening the door on the other side of which waited the cruel

fangs of the tiger!

But how much oftener had she seen him at the other door! How

in her grievous reveries had she gnashed her teeth and torn her hair when

she saw his start of rapturous delight as he opened the door of the lady!

How her soul had burned in agony when she had seen him rush to meet

that woman, with her flushing cheek and sparkling eye of triumph; when

she had seen him lead her forth, his whole frame kindled with the joy of

recovered life; when she had heard the glad shouts from the multitude,

and the wild ringing of the happy bells; when she had seen the priest, with his joyous followers, advance to the couple, and make them man and wife before her very eyes; and when she had seen them walk away together upon their path of flowers, followed by the tremendous shouts of the hilarious multitude, in which her one despairing shriek was lost and drowned!

Would it not be better for him to die at once, and go to wait for her in the blessed regions of semi-barbaric futurity?

And yet, that awful tiger, those shrieks, that blood!

Her decision had been indicated in an instant, but it had been made after days and nights of anguished deliberation. She had known she would be asked, she had decided what she would answer, and, without the slightest hesitation, she had moved her hand to the right.

The question of her decision is one not to be lightly considered, and it is not for me to presume to set myself up as the one person able to answer it. And so I leave it with all of you: Which came out of the opened door—the lady, or the tiger?

A CLOSER LOOK

When Frank Stockton sent "The Lady, or the Tiger?" to *Century* magazine

in 1882, it was called "In the King's Arena," after the setting of the tale.

The magazine's publisher thought that was too dull and concluded that

such an intriguing story demanded a more provocative title, so he changed

it to the familiar question that people know today. What the publisher did

not anticipate was that that question would be discussed everywhere,

among literary figures and readers of all classes. There was so much

demand for a firm answer that Stockton wrote a sequel called "The

Discourager of Hesitancy" in 1885. However, rather than providing any

definitive solution to the problem posed by the original tale, "The

Discourager of Hesitancy" presented yet another riddle that goes unsolved.

Stockton wanted his readers to examine the evidence for both

sides as it is presented in the story and to figure out the young man's fate

for themselves. Some would argue that Stockton provides many logical

A scene from the 2000 film *Gladiator*

clues supporting the choice of the tiger: Although she is said to have more

"force of character than anyone" (15), the princess is also a woman prone

to jealousy, and she perhaps allows her feelings to cloud her judgment.

The princess's quandary is that she has lost her lover for good, but she has

it in her power to choose who should have him instead—a vicious tiger that

will rip him to shreds or a beautiful woman who will marry him. Both would be binding and immediate consequences. One would end in certain death for him; the other would mean the death of love for her. After she learns the identity of the lady behind the door, she begins to improve upon her memory of the other woman: "Often she had seen, or imagined she had seen, this fair creature throwing glances of admiration upon the person of her lover, and sometimes she thought these glances were received and even returned" (15–16). Her blood boils at the thought of that woman marrying her lover. She contemplates that it would "be better for him to die at once," rather than marry the lady, "and go to wait for her in the blessed regions of semi-barbaric futurity" (19).

Yet the argument for love (and thus, the lady) is also a strong one. The princess is very much in love with this man, and their "souls are one" (16). She spends days and nights agonizing over how she will guide him in the arena, and she despairs at the idea of losing him to either the tiger or the woman. The very thought of the man she loves being devoured by a tiger horrifies her, and she cannot bear to picture the grisly scene of his

A captive tiger

death. She can, on the other hand, picture him much more easily choosing

the lady, being married right there in the arena, and leaving her to grieve

all alone. "But how much oftener had she seen him at the other door! How

in her grievous reveries had she gnashed her teeth and torn her hair when

she saw his start of rapturous delight as he opened the door of the lady!"

(18). This scenario seems much more realistic to the princess; pointing him

Royalty observing arena bloodsports

toward the door of the tiger would not do justice to their love, and she

would not be able to stomach such a decision: "And yet, that awful tiger,

those shrieks, that blood!" (19).

The evidence in favor of the tiger would seem to outweigh that for the lady, but the reader is still uncertain by the time the story comes to a close. For all the princess's "semi-barbaric" tendencies, many readers want to believe that she would allow her lover to live, thus allowing true, self-sacrificial love to triumph. When the princess's lover looks up at her from the arena floor to get her help in choosing the correct door, he believes that she will do what is best for him, trusting her implicitly because he knows her so well— or believes that he does. By following her silent advice to choose the door on the right, his decision is not a fair one—not even by the king's skewed definition of fairness. Yet the king cannot sacrifice his method of determining the fate of the accused; it is the established tradition. Besides, it will effectively remove the young man from his daughter's life, whichever door he chooses. As the man opens the door the princess has indicated "without the slightest hesitation" (17), the reader is left to ponder which fate she chose for her lover: the lady, or the tiger?

Frank Stockton

ABOUT THE AUTHOR

Frank Stockton grew up in a house that should have been ordered by religious piety, since his father, William Smith Stockton, was a highly regarded Methodist minister. But young Francis Richard was just as much of a firecracker as his fire-and-brimstone-preaching father—only his antics involved pranks instead of prayers. Born April 5, 1834, in Philadelphia, Pennsylvania, Stockton was free to run wild for the first 10 years of his life. But from 1844, when William retired, until 1860, the year of his death, young Frank felt bound by the iron clasp of his father's one-sided opinions.

Since his father was not in favor of his becoming a writer, Stockton studied wood engraving after high school and eventually set up his own office in New York City when he was 26. But his father's death set him free. That year, he married Marian E. Tuttle and wrote an eight-page pamphlet entitled *A Northern Voice for the Dissolution of the Union of* the United States of America. The tract was his futile attempt to prevent the impending Civil War, and it was his first and only endeavor to imitate the serious and overemotional voice of his preacher father. Changing styles, Stockton started writing for his brother John's newspaper. Then, in 1870, he published his first collection of children's fairy tales, *Ting-a-ling*. Stockton wanted to write fantasy stories for children because he felt that the moralizing tales that were available at the time were neither appealing nor effective; his fairy tales were popular because they were different: they were humorous and inventive, and they cleverly poked fun at human vices without preaching. To hone his skills, he also worked as an assistant editor at a magazine called *Hearth and Home* for six years. He then moved on to what would be an immensely popular children's publication called *St. Nicholas Magazine*. Although Stockton's failing eyesight caused him to resign from his editorial work at the magazine in 1878, he continued to write by dictating his thoughts to his wife or to a secretary.

The same year Stockton started work at *St. Nicholas* (1873), he also penned his first children's novel, *What Might Have Been Expected.*

Coming three years before Mark Twain's landmark *The Adventures of Tom Sawyer,* Stockton's book dealt with many of the same themes and misadventures of youthful characters, and indeed, the two authors were often compared to one another in terms of humorous style and subject matter. It took five long years of steady rejections before his first novel solely for adults, *Rudder Grange,* was finally published in 1879. Considering how long it took for Stockton to publish the tale of life on a canal boat, it was ironic that *Rudder Grange* became an instant best seller and remained one for more than 12 years. The book made Stockton famous and allowed him to concentrate on his writing full-time.

Optimistic about his future prospects, Stockton went abroad in search of a European publisher and new story material. Starting in 1882, the Stocktons traveled in Europe for two years; while they were there, Stockton's immortal short story "The Lady, or the Tiger?" appeared and had his fans clamoring for more. The public was mystified by the story's ambiguous ending; everyone wanted to know what was behind that door and what fateful choice the man had made. Stockton's only answer to inquisitive readers was frank and to the point: "If you decide which it was—the lady, or the tiger—you find out what kind of person you are yourself."

Although the story made Stockton famous, he eventually found it difficult to publish anything that was not in the same style or mode as "The Lady, or the Tiger?" Publishers wanted guaranteed success, and they wanted to capitalize on what had worked so well before. It took two years of frequent rejection, but he finally broke away from the mold in which he had been cast with the humorous tale "The Remarkable Wreck of the *Thomas Hyke*" in 1884.

In 1885, Marian recorded in her journal that new glasses enabled Stockton to begin "reading and writing a little, after three years' abstinence." That year saw the publication of his fairy tale "The Griffin and the Minor Canon," which was followed soon after by a gentle satire about a beekeeper's fantastical adventures called "The Bee-man of Orn."

The Stocktons occupied three homes over the course of their marriage, but the last was the best environment for the aging and ailing Frank. Located only a few miles away from where his mother grew up in Virginia, the peaceful setting of Claymont was ideal for rest and recuperation. While on his way back to Claymont from New York in 1902, Stockton stopped in Washington, D.C., for a banquet at the National Academy of Sciences on April 16. He became suddenly ill afterwards, though, and died in his hotel room of a cerebral hemorrhage on April 20, leaving behind a legacy that included a lady, a tiger, and much more.

Published by Creative Education

P.O. Box 227, Mankato, Minnesota 56002

Creative Education is an imprint of The Creative Company.

Design by Rita Marshall; production by Heidi Thompson

Page 20–31 text by Kate Riggs

Printed in the United States of America

Photographs by Alamy (Content Mine International), Corbis (Bettmann),

Getty Images (TEH ENG KOON/AFP)

Copyright © 2008 Creative Education

Illustrations © 2008 Etienne Delessert

Library of Congress Cataloging-in-Publication Data

Stockton, Frank Richard, 1834–1902.

The lady, or the tiger? / by Frank Stockton.

p. cm. — (Creative short stories)

Summary: A princess must choose the fate for her lover—the lady or the tiger.

ISBN 978-1-58341-583-2

[1. Choice—Fiction.] I. Title. II. Series.

PZ7.S866Lad 2008

[Fic]–dc22   2007008486

First edition

2 4 6 8 9 7 5 3 1